The Divorced Woman's Prayer Book

by

Ginger Farry

Paulist Press

NEW YORK MAHWAH

Library of Congress Cataloging-in-Publication Data

Farry, Ginger, 1941–
The divorced woman's prayer book / by Ginger Farry.
p. cm.
ISBN 0-8091-3320-2
1. Divorced women—Prayer-books and devotions—English. I. Title.
BV4596.D58F37 1992
242'.8433—dc20 92-10905
CIP

Published by Paulist Press
997 Macarthur Boulevard
Mahwah, New Jersey 07430

Printed and bound in the
United States of America

With love to
Michael and Eydi,
and thanks to
Father Jose Aquino
and prayers for all

FOREWORD

Divorce has now touched nearly every home and family in America. Divorce was once something "that happened to someone else." When it did happen, divorce was like an ugly family secret to be kept hidden. Often divorce was not discussed by the people to whom it happened, and certainly not by their parents and siblings. Because of shame and embarrassment, the untold stories of divorce remained locked in, like a skeleton hidden away. And as long as the stories remained untold, the divorce process could not be translated into any meaningful frame of reference. Without sharing the story of the divorce it was not possible for either the divorcing persons or those close to them to seek the help and support that is needed. Without a support system it is not likely that those touched by the divorce will grow through the experience and come to some new place of life.

In the early 1970s people who were experiencing the terror and confusion of divorce began coming together in groups to share their experiences and to offer loving support for one another. Their courage in initiating such a support system was the mechanism through which the divorce experience was articulated in such a manner that the nature of the process could be understood. In the ruins of broken marriages the keys to new life and possible growth were discovered.

The poet Robert Browning's words help clarify the value of the spoken and written words offered to others by men and women who have made their long and costly journey through divorce:

But, oh the things I learned from her
When sorrow walked with me.

The words of Ginger Farry are like a prism reflecting the many colors of the pain-filled process of grief that begins when marriages come apart. I find great power in the prayers of this divorced woman who has clearly walked the long and difficult road that was not spoken of in former times. In and through her agonizing quest for new life, Ginger Farry turns to God as the source and center of her hope. Because of her profound poetic ability, each prayer opened for me the wonder of human life that can offer strength to others by sharing the hurts of the heart. The author tells us what she learned when sorrow walked with her, and she does so in a way that invites each of her readers to allow sorrow to be a teaching companion for life.

Paula Ripple

Dear Reader:

For separated, divorced, and single parents of the world, sometimes there seems to be very little hope, not a lot to laugh about, and a near-impossible parenting job to perform. Dejected or rejected as we may now and again feel, we tend to forget that we can still count and lean heavily on the Lord.

When I first began writing *The Divorced Woman's Prayer Book*, it was simply my personal, conversational monologue with God—a group of poems which were in essence little prayers relating to the ever-changing stages that were part of my ten years as a single parent. I didn't know then where my copywriter's imagination, and the Lord, would lead me, and I certainly didn't expect that my whimsical yet earnest pleas would all be answered. I didn't realize, at the time, that what I was actually writing was a testimony and witness to the wonder of his ways. I was simply talking to God and reestablishing a relationship with him.

But he did hear—and respond. And these poem/prayers became the catalysts in my life. It was then I knew that I had to share them, and to share the experience of my healing with others—a small example of the mystery and power of his saving grace.

As you read what is here, I'm certain you will see the hurt, pain, anger and bitterness of what has been. You will also find some funny and unorthodox supplications as well—all indicative of my conversational manner of prayer. Yet I know that you, too, can find joy and comfort through communication with God in your personal journey toward spiritual growth. It is because of this sense of spiritual growth, that I recommend the poems be read in sequence. And I pray that as you read them, you will be filled with faith, find encouragement and inspiration, and learn to rely on his infinite compassion and love.

With praise to his holy name,

Ginger Farry

Someday

(A poem to my children)

How often I wondered what I'd leave you
someday
when I'm gone.
The gift of laughter, surely
and the gift of love.
The wisdom of my years,
in part, but not completely,
and in lieu of dollar value,
memories made of smiles.
Could this sustain you?
I feared not.
And then one of you asked about God
and showed the three of us the way—
the opportunity for a golden legacy
of faith
found in prayer.
And I cried in joy.

My heart pours forth a good word: I speak my poem to the king; my tongue is the pen of the swift writer.

Psalm 44:2

No one to follow, Lord
Did you mean it to be this way?
No one to lean on Lord
And I need to lean today.
No one to talk to, Lord
But wait, we're talking now!
I've someone to follow, Lord
If you'll only show me how.

They miss their dad
I know they do
but then sometimes
I miss him too.
Though we're a unit
just we three
it's hard to be
a family;
and difficult to
keep a home
when a mother's
all alone.
And all the chores
that I can't shirk,
like helping kids
with their homework
make days and nights
go racing by
with hardly any
time to cry,
or sing or talk
or laugh or sleep
for fears and worries
always creep
into my head
while anger grows
and teardrops fall
but no one knows.
Except you, Lord,
for you can see

all joy and all
adversity.
So please, dear God
just keep me strong
to teach my children
right from wrong
And help them learn
and give them love
And show them there's a
Lord above
who unlike Mom
is so sublime
He can listen to all
at the very same time.

The Lord is my chalice,
my loving cup.
The world is my child
and it's spitting up.
My life is a song
being sung off-key,
for I haven't yet mastered
the melody.
Oh, Lord, let me hear the sound of your psalms,
that lead me to peace in your loving arms,
and give me the strength to follow your way—
no matter what happens to me today.

Step by step
you're taking me closer to you and I thank you.
Step by step
you're helping me to know
that though I stumble and my walk's uncertain,
you understand and steady me as I go.

I hoped, I hoped in the Lord, and he stooped down to me, and he heard my cry. And he drew me out of the pit of destruction, from the mire of the swamp, and he set my feet upon a rock, he made firm my steps.

Psalm 39:2–3

A loveless day
is there such a thing?
When nothing goes right
and the phone doesn't ring?
Not a word from a friend
not a new date in view
then the T.V. breaks down
and the vacuum goes too.
Just a hill of repairs,
lots of errands to run
and my daughter is late
and I can't find my son.
And I look for some comfort,
assistance–a break
but the kids arrive home
and they just seem to take.
'Cause both want a ride
to meet with their friends:
diverse destinations
at opposite ends!
One says, "drive me
downtown to a show"
and the other "me first
'cause I'm late, you know."
And I just want to scream
and run out the door–
quit being a Mom

and collapse on the floor.
Yes, a day like today
would be loveless indeed
if I didn't have Jesus
to quiet my need.

Revised Menu

I made boeuf Bourguignon tonight
the kids complained with cries:
What is this stuff we can't pronounce?
It's not for folks our size!
I told them about China
and places far away
but they just wouldn't listen, Lord
and I didn't know what else to say.
I guess they had a point to make
though the food was hardly "bad"
—they're more a hot dog bunch, you see,
the boeuf belonged to Dad!

In Again/Out Again Mom

The children are bedded down, my Lord
the sitter will soon arrive.
And in again/out again Mom
is about to come alive.
It's off to a local chapter
*of dear P.W.P.**
Where hopefully I will dance and smile
and someone will talk to me.
I pray, Lord, that you'll guide me.
I pray, indeed I weep
that the sitter will come, and I'll get out
before I fall asleep.

*Parents Without Partners

I know I must speak about bitterness, Lord.
It's a thorn that forever pricks me.
I recognize my weakness.
Please replace it with faith in thee.

Still bitter, Lord,
the thorns still dig.
How about it, Lord?
Would you toss me a fig?

"Ask, and it shall be given you; seek, and you shall find; knock, and it shall be opened to you. For everyone who asks, receives; and he who seeks, finds; and to him who knocks, it shall be opened. Or what man is there among you, who, if his son asks him for a loaf, will hand him a stone; or if he asks for a fish, will hand him a serpent? Therefore, if you, evil as you are, know how to give good gifts to your children, how much more will your Father in heaven give good things to those who ask him!"

Matthew 7:7–11

Our needs are very simple, Lord
just shelter, food and clothes,
some money for the dentist,
nasal spray for my son's nose,
galoshes for both children,
warm coats for winter's chills,
small payments for our creditors,
and for my ulcer pills.

So please, Lord, give me patience
every time I must behold
a pair of worn out sneakers
that are only two weeks old.
And I won't ask for riches,
not a talent or a cent,
not for shoes or clothes or Calvins
nor our ever-rising rent.

Just patience, peace and charity
for all I love and know
and especially, dear Jesus,
for everyone I owe.

We didn't take time for grace tonight,
we three ate on the bed.
Yes, plates in hand, the T.V. on—
I had to get them fed!

I worked so late, was almost eight,
I know you'll surely see
It's not that we weren't grateful, Lord:
just incredibly hungry!

Thoughts on the Run

Lord, please let the car start tomorrow . . .
let the washing machine complete two more
cycles . . .
find me the strength of Samson to bring down the
storms . . .
and help me to finish those medical forms.

It's Halloween day
and I sit by the door
handing out candy
and goodies galore.

Yes, my children insisted,
to be out on their own,
'cause they're old enough now
to leave mother at home.

And I thank you dear Lord,
And give praise to your name,
for love that is constant
and always the same.

And if you wouldn't mind,
I have one request—quick—
may they not eat their whole loot
and make themselves sick!

Have no anxiety, but in every prayer and supplication with thanksgiving let your petitions be made known to God.

Philippians 4:6

Tonight I'm hungry for you, Lord
I need to feel your grace.
Tonight I covet you, my God,
and long for your embrace.
I've folded all the children's wash,
put all their things away.
I've changed the sheets and ironed their clothes,
it's been a busy day.
Tomorrow morn it's back to work,
the weekend's all but through
but goodness I'm so tired, Lord,
and I just don't know what to do.
The news is so depressing, too,
the world is such a mess,
and here I am with mundane cares,
I'm guilty, I confess.
Oh, please, Lord, won't you hear my knock,
gently on your door.
Yes, I'm aware I'm needed
but you're needed so much more.
So please, take my anxieties
and heal me of my fear
and when—like now—I'm most alone,
help me recall you're here.

He doesn't see the children much,
no matter how they plead
and I have tried to give my all
to fill their every need.
At first I found it difficult
when we just numbered 3
but now we're 4 again, dear Lord
—it's you, the kids, and me!

Lord, help me to love them today
As they bicker, fight and brawl.
Help me to teach them peace and joy
Won't you hear my call?
Silence all their sibling screams,
Accept this prayerful poem–
for I've no option to recite:
"Wait till Dad comes home."

Give me extra strength, dear Lord
for as flowers need their stem,
this mother needs some wisdom–
so please, help me, help them.

My daughter is unhappy, Lord.
A friend has hurt her so.
I know just what she's feeling
but my words can't heal her blow.
Please help me find a way, dear Lord
to somehow ease her pain
so she'll forgive, forget and be
a smiling child again.

"Thou shalt love the Lord thy God with thy whole heart, and with thy whole soul, and with thy whole mind. This is the greatest and the first commandment. And the second is like it, Thou shalt love thy neighbor as thyself."

Matthew 22:34-39

It's hard to love my neighbor, Lord
when sometimes I can see,
a distant glance, that condescends
and labels: divorcee.
You'd think because the world has changed
and many share my plight
that folks might treat us naturally
and not be so uptight.
But even friends are sometimes cruel
though it is not their plan.
For after all, instinctively,
a woman "guards" her man.
So I've become "temptation"
and I'm not asked to tea,
Oh, Lord, please send a single friend
to keep me company.

There's anger in my heart today,
I pray you'll take it all away;
for I had thought that love was mine,
and I'd given so much time
to love and cherish and obey
while he looked another way.

Now, Lord, please help me let it go
to look toward you because you know
the way to channel hurt and fears,
and still the rage of silent tears.
Ease this anger that I feel,
and help my frightened heart to heal.

Wishing . . .

Wishing, Lord
for a better job,
snow tires,
the money to pay for new glasses,
my child support check to arrive,
a pleasant date,
quieter children,
and a new couch for the living room;
I suppose
is wrong.
So all frivolity aside–
you decide.

May no temptation take hold of you but such as man is equal to. God is faithful and will not permit you to be tempted beyond your strength, but with the temptation will also give you a way out that you may be able to bear it.

I Corinthians 10:13

The door fell off the car today,
the mechanic was so surprised.
And I just stared and laughed out loud
before his very eyes.
It wasn't what I thought was wrong,
it was a new repair.
I'd asked for just a safety check—
please let the bill be fair!
I had to take the bus to work
and leave the car behind.
I pray he'll fix the car okay;
good mechanics are hard to find.

Merry Christmas/Moody Blues

I'm lonely, Lord
not missing him,
just all alone
and wanting in
on joy and laughter
two can share
as a loving part
of a happy pair.
We could sing carols
in the snow
or sit beside
the fire's glow
or shop together
for that big surprise
to help light up
our children's eyes.
And wrapping gifts
is just no fun
when all the wrapping's
done by one.
So Lord, I pray
could you please send
a special
Christmas season friend
to ease the burden
half the way
and help to celebrate your day!

I've forgiven, Lord
I've stopped placing blame
and when some were surprised
I just mentioned your name.

I thank you, Lord
you've set me free,
that's one more thing
you've done for me.

I'm going out again, dear Lord
to make another start,
I thank you for the light and joy
you've placed within my heart
And now I think I'll really see
Your face in all mankind
and maybe then I'll get to know
the love I'm meant to find.

For how dost thou know, O wife, whether thou wilt save thy husband? Or how dost thou know, O husband, whether thou wilt save thy wife? . . . And the unmarried woman, and the virgin, thinks about the things of the Lord, that she may be holy in body and in spirit. Whereas she who is married thinks about the things of the world, how she may please her husband.

I Corinthians 7:16, 34

A new kind of swinging single, Lord
is what I want to be.
I recognize my wants and needs,
my sexuality.
But all these gifts you gave us
are not to be misused
and certainly, I've erred Lord,
your mercy I've abused.
Yes, Lord, I am a sinner
and I beg you pardon me
for actions that have reigned above
responsibility.
Though pleasure is not evil
and in itself is good
it's just one aspect of a life
to be placed where it should.
Enhance my life with truth, Lord
let not instinct be my guide
for physical attraction
is just the sensual side.
Let my swinging hold the rhythm
of your holy drummer's beat
and let the spirit move me, Lord
and lift me off my feet.
Guide me and assist me
in this world that moves so fast—
for my pulsing heart already knows
a love that will always last!

Just when I think I've got it down pat
Yes, just when I think I know where it's at
something occurs, pulling me under
Oh, Lord, please forgive my miserable blunder.
Though I tried hard to see you in each one today
I lost my perspective and drifted away
God, give me the grace to slow down and see
that indeed it's you who live in me.
And when I am foolish,
discouraged or blue,
I'll never be blinded
if my eyes are on you!

The dog chewed up the carpet.
The cat sprayed on the chair.
I'll get another carpet, Lord,
put the cat in for "repair."
I bought the kids their Easter clothes.
I got a raise in pay.
I had a "big" date Friday night—
looks like a lovely day.
We'll sing in church tomorrow
and thank you for the keys
that help us sort our problems
and find priorities.

Embrace

I used to look for him in crowds,
along the beach
or even at a bar.
I used to hope he'd show up soon
white charger or not,
prince or pauper.
And I was frightened he might not exist
—and scared of spending my life alone.
And now I've found Him, my Prince
though He was always there.
He was waiting for me to discard
my empty search,
find fulfillment in His word
and let Him lead.
Now His glory fills me with peace
His love with joy
and His pain for we sinners of the world
with sorrow.
Now
as I walk through His church,
I can see for the first time
the stations that were His torment
and my eyes glisten with tears.
Jesus, Lord,
I didn't know
I was always in your arms.

My son returned from school today
And he shouted loud
"I ran two miles in record time
Oh, boy, the coach was proud."

I smiled congratulations,
and then, a look conveyed,
made me ask him how he did it—
and he floored me with
"I prayed."

Now it came to pass as they were on their journey, that he entered a certain village; and a woman named Martha welcomed him to her house. And she had a sister called Mary, who also seated herself at the Lord's feet, and listened to his word. But Martha was busy about much serving. And she came up and said, "Lord, is it no concern of thine that my sister has left me to serve, alone? Tell her therefore to help me." But the Lord answered and said to her. "Martha, Martha, thou art anxious and troubled about many things; and yet only one thing is needful. Mary has chosen the best part, and it will not be taken away from her."

Luke 10:38–42

I'm learning to live alone, my God
I'm learning to like it too
I'm learning to make the best of it
for there's so much I can do.
I can wear my hair in curlers
I can play my music loud
I can choose a quiet evening
or invite a joyous crowd
I can say "let's eat McDonald's"
when cooking seems a plight
I can leave the bedroom light on
and read all through the night
I can let the house get messy
and ponder silly schemes
or sit around and write a poem
—indulge in sweet daydreams
I can give my children all my love
and they will surely see
that as I learn to grow in you
they learn and grow with me!

How wonderfully you fit, Lord in the rhythms of my life

How wonderfully you fit, Lord
in the rhythms of my life,
Now that I walk with you daily
Now that I sit quietly holding your hand,
reading your psalms,
Now that I caress my children
and share with them the joy of your love,
the peace of your words,
How wonderfully I fit, Lord
in the rhythms of my life.

Dear Mary, blessed mother mine,
I thank you for the gift of time
that makes a mother wise and strong
and gives her courage to go on.
I prayed to you in early years,
you were my fortress through childhood fears,
I ask you now to guide my flock
to keep hearts open—
but the front door locked;
while I'm at work, please keep an eye,
Oh, blessed Mary, won't you try
for surely you can understand
the sadness and the awe at hand
for when they took your son from you
You were a single parent too.

I have taken joys to you
I have taken sorrows too
And now at last my spirit's free
and I offer: poetry.
Take these words Lord, if you will
spread them over rock and hill.
Let them solace all who mourn,
may in their rhythms, faith be born
and should they comfort any cry,
Lord, I'll know it's you
not I.

I'm content, Lord
whatever my fate
for I found you
to contemplate.

Amen.